NATIONAL GEOGRAPHIC

T0061130

Where Is It Going?

Lee Scott

Where is it going?

37

Where is it going?

Where is it going?

AMBULANCE ONLY
PED
XING
10
MPH
EMERGENCY
ROOM
ENTRANCE
AMBULANCE
ENTRANCE
ONLY
Memorial Hospital
Service

Where is it going?

Where is it going?